Sleeping Beauty
The Story of the Ballet

Written by Laurie Sale • Illustrated by Linda Hill Griffith

Andrews and McMeel
A Universal Press Syndicate Company
Kansas City

ISBN: 0-8362-0640-1

Library of Congress Catalog Card Number: 93-71008

To Bob and Lauren for their support and patience. —L.H.G.

Special thanks to Frank McGrath and the editorial and production
staff at Andrews and McMeel.

Sleeping Beauty

The Story of the Ballet

nce, long ago, a King and Queen were very sad. They had everything they wanted except a baby. They asked advice from members of the royal court, but the King and Queen were feeling like their dream would never come true. Many years passed, and then, one day, the Queen joyfully announced that a baby was on the way. Soon, a beautiful baby named Princess Aurora was born. The King and Queen were delighted.

The King and Queen celebrated the birth of their baby by inviting everyone they knew to the royal christening party. Among the invited guests were six fairies who each brought an extra-special gift for Princess Aurora. As the fairies danced around the new princess, each came forward and presented Aurora with a gift.

The Fairy of the Woodland Glades gave Aurora the gift of dance, so that she might dance as gracefully as a feather.

The Fairy of the Enchanted Garden gave Aurora the gift of beauty, so that she would be as beautiful as a delicate flower.

The Fairy of the Songbirds gave Aurora the gift of song, so that she could sing as sweetly as the birds.

The Fairy of the Crystal Fountain
gave Aurora the gift of music, so that
she could play all kinds of musical
instruments exquisitely.

The Fairy of the Golden Vine gave
Aurora the gift of happiness, so
that she would always be happy
and could make others happy too.

But before the last of the six fairies,
the Lilac Fairy, could present her gift to the
Princess, a clap of loud thunder announced
the appearance of an uninvited guest.

A dark chariot being drawn by large black rats appeared, carrying a very angry and wicked fairy named Carabosse *(ka-ra-boss)*. Carabosse was outraged that she had not been invited to the royal christening, and so instead of a gift, she put a curse on the baby Princess. "You will grow up to be beautiful, but you will not live long," she pronounced. "Someday, unexpectedly, you will prick your finger, and then you will die." Her evil laughter filled the room, and with that she was gone.

The King and Queen were overcome with sadness. It was the Lilac Fairy who made them stop crying. She explained, "I can't stop the evil curse that Carabosse put on Princess Aurora, but I can lessen it. The Princess will indeed grow up to be beautiful, but when she pricks her finger she will not die. Instead she and the royal court will fall asleep for a hundred years, and then the spell will be broken when a brave Prince kisses the Princess." As she left, the Lilac Fairy hugged the Princess and everyone felt relieved.

Even though the Lilac Fairy had changed the curse, the King decided to take extra precautions to protect his daughter. He ordered his soldiers to collect and destroy every needle, pin, and spindle in the kingdom. He had everything removed that might be able to prick the Princess's finger.

Many years went by and Princess Aurora grew up to be a beautiful young woman. She was also a graceful and talented dancer. Her parents were very proud of her, and for her sixteenth birthday decided to give her a spectacular party. They invited many guests, including four very handsome Princes. The King and Queen hoped that their daughter would fall in love and marry one of the young men. Each Prince presented Aurora with a red rose, and as she danced gracefully with each of them, she realized that none of them was the man of her dreams.

Aurora danced the night away. Toward the end of the party, a strange old woman appeared. She had been waiting out of sight, until Aurora was alone, and now came over to her and presented her with a gift. It was something that the Princess had never seen before . . . a spindle. As she looked at it, she accidentally pricked her finger. She tried to find her father and tell him what had happened, but she felt too sleepy.

Unable to move or speak, Princess Aurora curled up on the floor and fell fast asleep. The King and Queen were terrified. Suddenly, the strange old woman took off her disguise. It was the wicked fairy, Carabosse! She cackled her wicked laugh, as the frightened King and Queen carried their precious daughter off to her bedroom.

Luckily, the Lilac Fairy was also at Aurora's birthday party. Many years earlier, the Lilac Fairy had made a promise to change the evil Carabosse's curse. She waved her wand, and everyone in the royal court fell peacefully asleep.

A hundred years went by as everyone in the royal court slept. The once beautiful garden grew full of large trees, and thorny vines covered the castle until it was impossible to see the castle from the woods.

One day in the woods, not too far from the palace, a handsome young Prince named Florimund was hunting. As he approached a small pond, he was amazed at the vision that he saw. A beautiful, giant seashell came gliding across the water toward him, carrying the Lilac Fairy. The Lilac Fairy explained to Prince Florimund about the spell that had been cast a hundred years earlier, and how it could only be broken by the kiss from a gallant Prince.

As the Lilac Fairy spoke, she waved her wand and the Prince was able to see a vision of the sleeping Princess. He fell in love immediately and knew his kiss could bring Aurora back to life. Florimund and the Lilac Fairy sailed off in the boat toward the castle.

Prince Florimund and the Lilac Fairy reached the castle and had to make their way through all the cobwebs and dust that now filled the castle. As they went from room to room looking for Princess Aurora, the Prince was surprised to see that everyone in the court was sound asleep.

Finally the Prince found the Princess's bedroom. She looked even more lovely than he had imagined. He knew that his love for her was real. He knelt down by her side and kissed her gently. Slowly the Princess opened her eyes, and saw the most handsome man she had ever seen. She knew instantly that he was the man of her dreams.

The Prince had broken the spell! The King and Queen and all the members of the royal court woke up. Since they had been asleep for such a long time, there was a lot of work to be done. Everyone began to dust, clean up the cobwebs, and make the castle look like it had before.

The Prince and Princess were in love and decided to get married. The King and Queen were delighted. It was the loveliest wedding that anyone in the kingdom had ever seen. All of Aurora's childhood friends were invited:

Puss in Boots and the White Cat,

Little Red Riding Hood and the Wolf,

Cinderella and Prince Charming,

and Bluebird with his Princess.

Princess Aurora and Prince Florimund were the happiest and most beautiful bride and groom. They really loved each other and lived together, happily, ever after. The Lilac Fairy was one of their closest friends, and no one ever heard of the wicked fairy Carabosse, again.

Sleeping Beauty was first presented in St. Petersburg, Russia, over one hundred years ago. The King of Russia and many of his court attended this gala opening. The music for *Sleeping Beauty* was written by Peter Ilyich Tchaikovsky *(peter il-ee-ich chie-koff-skee)*, one of the most famous Russian composers, who also wrote the music for the ballets *Swan Lake* and *The Nutcracker*. It took Tchaikovsky a little more than a year to compose the music for *Sleeping Beauty*. Marius Petipa *(mahr-ee-us puh-tee-pah)* created the choreography to go along with Tchaikovsky's music, and many ballet companies still use his dance directions today.

Since its introduction in Russia so many years ago, *Sleeping Beauty* has remained a favorite among ballet lovers the world over.